SIMPLE MACHINES

WHEEL AND AXLE

ARE MACHINES

DOUGLAS BENDER

A Crabtree Roots Plus Book

CRABTREE
Publishing Company
www.crabtreebooks.com

School-to-Home Support for Caregivers and Teachers

This book helps children grow by letting them practice reading. Here are a few guiding questions to help the reader with building his or her comprehension skills. Possible answers appear here in red.

Before Reading:

- What do I think this book is about?
    - *I think this book is about wheels and axles.*
    - *I think this book is about how useful wheels and axles are in our lives.*
- What do I want to learn about this topic?
    - *I want to learn when wheels and axles were invented.*
    - *I want to learn things I can do with wheels and axles.*

During Reading:

- I wonder why...
    - *I wonder why the axle keeps the wheel in place.*
    - *I wonder why wind turbines use wheels and axles.*
- What have I learned so far?
    - *I have learned that a car uses four wheels and two axles.*
    - *I have learned that a wheelbarrow uses an axle and one wheel to help people move things.*

After Reading:

- What details did I learn about this topic?
    - *I have learned that the axle turns the wheel or wheels.*
    - *I have learned that a wind turbine helps us make energy from the wind.*
- Read the book again and look for the vocabulary words.
    - *I see the word **wheelbarrow** on page 16 and the word **energy** on page 20. The other vocabulary words are found on page 23.*

This is a **wheel and axle**.

Pulley

Lever

Screw

It is one of six
simple machines.

Wedge

Inclined Plane

Wheel and Axle

Simple machines have few or no moving parts.

axle

The axle goes through
the center of the wheel.

It turns the wheel.

The axle also keeps
the wheel in place.

Wheels and axles help us move things.

Some wheels and axles are big.

They can move larger
and heavier objects.

Some wheels and
axles are small.

A car has four wheels and two axles.

A **wheelbarrow** uses an axle and wheel to help us move things.

Wind turbines use wheels and axles.

Wind turbines help us make **energy** from the wind.

Word List
Sight Words

a	is	to
an	keeps	two
and	make	us
are	move	use
big	moving	uses
can	no	
car	or	
few	parts	
four	place	
from	small	
has	some	
help	the	
helps	things	
in	this	

Words to Know

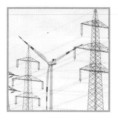

energy

simple machines

wheelbarrow

wheel and axle

wind turbines

Written by: Douglas Bender
Designed by: Rhea Wallace
Series Development: James Earley
Proofreader: Janine Deschenes
Production coordinator
    and Prepress technician: Katherine Berti
Print coordinator: Katherine Berti
Educational Consultant: Marie Lemke M.Ed.

Photographs:
Shutterstock: pio3: cover, p. 3; tatui suwat: p. 3, 23; Talk:
    p. 6; Zarya Maxium: p. 7; Alexandrovich: p. 8; Kiev.
    Victor: p. 9; Natalie Jean: p. 11; Mike Flippo: p. 12-13;
    ok_kate: p. 14; Giovanni Love: p. 15; Feeling Lucky: p.
    17, 23; pedrosala: p. 19, 23; Ivanova Tetyana: p. 21, 23

SIMPLE MACHINES

WHEELS AND AXLES
ARE MACHINES

Library and Archives Canada
Cataloguing in Publication

CIP available at Library and Archives Canada

Library of Congress
Cataloging-in-Publication Data

CIP available at Library of Congress

Crabtree Publishing Company

www.crabtreebooks.com   1-800-387-7650   Printed in the U.S.A./CG20210915/012022

In Canada: We acknowledge the financial support of the Government of Canada through the
Canada Book Fund for our publishing activities.

Published in the United States
Crabtree Publishing
347 Fifth Avenue, Suite 1402-145
New York, NY, 10016

Published in Canada
Crabtree Publishing
616 Welland Ave.
St. Catharines, ON, L2M 5V6